D1369566

101 Celtic
spirals

745 .4 DAV
Davis, Courtney, 1946-
101 Celtic spirals /

PALM BEACH COUNTY
LIBRARY SYSTEM
3650 Summit Boulevard
West Palm Beach, FL 33406-4198

101 Celtic
spirals

courtney davis

David and Charles

A DAVID & CHARLES BOOK

David & Charles is a subsidiary of F+W (UK) Ltd.,
an F+W Publications Inc. company

First published in the UK in 2005

Copyright © Courtney Davis 2005

Distributed in North America
by F+W Publications, Inc.
4700 East Galbraith Road
Cincinnati, OH 45236
1-800-289-0963

Courtney Davis has asserted his right to be identified as
author of this work in accordance with the Copyright,
Designs and Patents Act, 1988.

All rights reserved. No part of this publication may be
reproduced, stored in a retrieval system, or transmitted, in
any form or by any means, electronic or mechanical, by
photocopying, recording or otherwise, without prior
permission in writing from the publisher.

Readers are permitted to reproduce any of the patterns or
designs in this book for their personal use and without the
prior permission of Courtney Davis. Any use of the patterns
or designs for charitable or commercial purposes is not
permitted without the prior permission of Courtney Davis.

A catalogue record for this book is available from the
British Library.

ISBN 0 7153 1775 X

Printed in Singapore by KHL Printing Co.Pte Ltd
for David & Charles
Brunel House   Newton Abbot   Devon

Commissioning Editor   Neil Baber
Editor   Jennifer Proverbs
Art Editor   Mike Moule
Designer   Jodie Lystor
Production Controller   Kelly Smith

This book is dedicated to Sandra and Terry at
Best of Europe and Jennie from Seren who have
been a great support and inspiration while I
was working on this book.

Visit our website at **www.davidandcharles.co.uk**

David & Charles books are available from all good
bookshops; alternatively you can contact our Orderline on
(0)1626 334555 or write to us at FREEPOST EX2 110,
David & CharlesDirect, Newton Abbot, TQ12 4ZZ (no
stamp required UK mainland).

contents

introduction

The spiral is a natural pattern of growth that we see time and again in nature. It is, therefore, perhaps no surprise that we find spiral designs are among the earliest examples of Celtic art, and indeed spiral designs are to be found in the art of most early cultures. It is the only decorative motif used in Christian Celtic art that demonstrably has its roots in the preceding pagan period.

One-coiled spirals can be found in the art of most of the peoples of Europe, Asia, Africa, Polynesia and the Americas and some of the very earliest examples dating from between 25,000BC and 15,000BC have been found engraved on mammoth ivory in the Ukraine and in Yugoslavia. It was the Celts who much later developed the method of making two, three and four or more coils and developed the three or four-armed spiral designs that are so characteristically Celtic. The best early examples are to be found on stone monuments such as the famous megalithic site of Newgrange in Ireland. Dating to about 3,200BC it contains 97 large stones piled up at the bottom of a large mound, many of which bear beautifully carved designs of spirals, lozenges, zigzags, and other symbols. The most famous of these is the stone marking the entrance with its carvings of a triple spiral, double spirals, concentric semi-circles and lozenges, which are similar to those found in Gavrinis, Brittany. The tri-spiral designs of three linked spirals are particularly unusual at Newgrange.

Early Celtic Cultures

Before the emergence of what most of us recognise as Celtic art in the 5th century BC, the ancestors of the Celts were the people of the Urnfield culture, so-called because they buried their dead in cremation urns. Between 1,200 and 700BC, they spread west from their eastern European homeland into the area of modern Austria, Germany, Switzerland and France. From here, their culture developed into a recognizably Celtic form called the *Hallstatt* after a village in Austria where archaeologists have discovered many important objects. In this period, the Celtic economy was based upon the extraction and sale of salt. Their metalwork was also in great demand as the innovative Celtic blacksmiths had embraced the art of working in iron and produced the best metal goods in Europe. The term 'Celt' was coined by the ancient Greeks around this time, who called the barbarian peoples they traded with *Keltoi*. The Celts, however, were never one nation ruled by a single commander but always a broad and loose cultural-linguistic group, and the area where they lived was a constantly changing collection of tribes.

Another important archaeological site, *La Tène* (meaning the shallows) is beside Lake Neuchatel in Switzerland and it gives its name to the next identifiable style in early Celtic art. Most of the richest and most characteristic material of this period has been found in a hundred or so barrow graves further north in the middle Rhine area. The characteristic art of the *La Tène* is non-representational, non-naturalistic and even abstract in style. Lotus flowers, foliage and three- or four-leafed palmettes are found on a variety of objects. At this time the spiral seems to have been the favoured ornamental pattern of the Celtic warrior and chieftain. It was applied as a surface decoration to items such as shields, helmets, sword sheaths, armlets, horse trappings and other personal ornaments. Often elaborate in character, they testify to an amazing expertise in metalworking. The spiral may also have been the preferred style of decoration for a warrior to paint on himself before battle.

With the flowering of the *La Tène* culture in Germany and Switzerland, the presence of spirals on the stone monuments left by previous peoples may have provided a source of inspiration for their craftsmen. These simple one-coil spirals on early monuments must have inspired the later Celtic developments, which were generally more elaborate and usually radiated out from a centre of three or four lines, forming a triskele (a three-legged motif, best-known from the three leg emblem of the Isle of Man) or a swastika at the heart of the spiral.

The Celts in Britain

As far as it is known, Celtic peoples began arriving in mainland Britain in about 600BC and succeeded in introducing their language and culture to the people of the entire British Isles. Some would have been from the *Hallstatt* culture and others from *La Tène*, both teaching their crafts and art forms to the natives. They brought new refinements to spiral design work, which now used S or C shapes to link their spirals (the C-shape is closely related to the 'pelta' motif, which has been likened in its appearance to a cross-section of a mushroom with its cap curling under). The type of spiral decoration known as 'mirror style' has a characteristic basketry hatching infill and examples have been found on scabbards and spears, as well as on the backs of a few dozen bronze mirrors dating from around the early first century.

After the 2nd century, Celtic art effectively died out in Britain to be revived several hundred years later in the 5th century with the production of brooches, hanging bowls, and other objects. This revival in the new Celtic Christian era represents a separate tradition from that of the *La Tène* Celts, and it was readily absorbed by the craftsman in Ireland who refined it and took it to its greatest heights. The objects decorated in the new Christian tradition are mainly ecclesiastical and include metal reliquaries, stone crosses and stone slabs decorated with crosses. The best spiral designs on these sculptured stone monuments are to be found in Ireland and Scotland and, more rarely, in Wales, Cornwall and the Isle of Man. Typical examples of spiral ornament may be seen on the sculptured monuments in Ireland at Kells, Co. Meath; Monasterboice, Co. Louth; Clonmacnois, Co. Offaly; and Kilklispeen cemetery, Co. Kilkenny. In Scotland they can be found at Nigg, Shandwick and Hilton of Cadboll, all in Ross-shire; the Maiden Stone, Aberdeenshire; St. Vigeans, Angus; Meigle and Dunfallandy House, Pitlochry in Perthshire; and Ardchattan, near Oban, Argyll. The spiral ornament is less common in metalwork than in the manuscripts, although fine examples of the skills of the Celtic metalworker can be seen on the Ardagh Chalice, Tara Brooch, Hunterston Brooch, the Monymusk Reliquary and the Athlone Crucifixion Plaque.

The first example of a spiral decoration in manuscript illumination is to be found in the *Book of Durrow*, written around 680 it is the earliest of the surviving, fully illuminated Gospel books. Measuring 245 x 145mm (9¾ x 5¾in) in size it contains canon tables, carpet pages, full page pictures of the symbols of the evangelists, and all the different types of ornamentation that we recognize as Celtic art. The ornaments show that the artist had drawn upon several widely different sources for his inspiration. Scrolls and spirals are derived directly from the tradition represented by some of the latchets and brooches and from the 7th-century hanging-bowls. One whole carpet page is devoted to spirals – tight outer coils of hair-fine lines which curve inward to fill the void with smaller scrolls – linked by curved expanded trumpet-shapes at the ends. These terminals meet in small pointed ovoid motifs picked out in a contrasting colour. The spiral was also used by the artist to create highly decorative illuminated lettering, the terminals of each letter bursting into colourful spiral and trumpet patterns, and curvilinear forms with a rotating movement. In comparison to the *Book of Durrow* the illumination in the slightly later *Gospel of Saint Willibrord* is more refined and the spiral terminals have a much finer line and end with a new type of spiral with squeezed sides that jut out like a flag.

Creating Spirals

There are clear signs that give us a clue as to the construction methods of some of the decoration within the Gospel books, where dry point layouts and the use of a compass and ruler can easily be seen. Hair spirals, which were an important element of the manuscript art of the seventh and eighth century, could only have been created freehand, though even by turning the folio spirals it would still have been very difficult to draw, not to mention keeping the thickness of the line even. (A folio is one half of a bifolia – a double sheet of vellum which when folded forms a quire.) Brushes and pens with widths of varying fineness were used and the painting may have been done with brushes made from marten fur. No instruments have been found that may have helped in their construction, though some scholars suggest that crystals may have been used to magnify the work, although they would probably have introduced an element of distortion.

Naturally enough the famous illuminated manuscripts provide some of the richest and most sophisticated Celtic spiral designs. The best examples of these can be found in the *Book of Durrow*, the *Gospel of St Willibrord*, the *Lindisfarne Gospels*, the *Gospels of St. Chad*, the *Gospels of St. Gall*, the *Book of Armagh*, The *Book of Kells* and the *Gospels of MacRegal*. Judging from the evidence afforded by the dated specimens of surviving manuscripts, the best kind of spiral ornament seems to have disappeared entirely from Christian Celtic art after the first quarter of the 10th century, making the spiral design not only the earliest decorative ornament to be used in Celtic art but also the first to disappear.

Modern spiral design

Knotwork is the ornament that people instantly recognize as being Celtic and it is used, often crudely, in logos and illustrations when a Celtic theme is required. Unfortunately the mechanics and intricacies of knotwork construction is not always appreciated, although understanding of it is growing, but apart from Celtic connoisseurs, the real appreciation and use of the Celtic spiral is still a long way off. To most people the spiral decoration is secondary to knotwork but it is, to my mind, more satisfying to work with, its potent power coming from its continued use through thousands of years and by many different cultures. In modern Celtic design it symbolizes the movement of the spirit through different experiences: spinning into the center of the whorl and then catapulting out again to journey on a different path. It can be seen as the continuation of life from birth, death and re-birth as it did so many centuries ago for the Celtic warrior who adorned his armour and himself with spiral patterns before going into battle, knowing that a hero's death meant resurrection to the world of heroes in the Celtic otherworld.

The development of this organic design from the simplest of coiled spirals carved in stone to the complex designs found in illuminated manuscripts make this a versatile symbol which can be used in a variety of ways to add decoration.

designs
in stone

Section of spiral ornament dated around 2,500 BC. *Tumulus at Newgrange,*
Co. Meath, Ireland

Labyrinth design from a carved rock face, possibly Bronze Age. *Rocky Valley, Cornwall*

designs in stone

Decoration from a sandstone pillar statue from 4th–3rd-century BC. *Waldenbuch,*
Kr. Böbliingen, Germany

From a carved granite pillar dated between the 1st-century BC and the 1st-century.
Turoe, Co. Galway, Ireland

Carved stone from Mullaghmast, County Kildare. *National Museum of Ireland, Dublin*

Spiral design carved on the early 8th-century Aberlemno Cross Slab.
Aberlemno, Angus, Scotland

Spiral decoration from an early 8th-century Scottish stone cross.

designs in stone

Taken from a panel on the 8th-century North Cross at Ahenny.
Ahenny, Co. Tipperary, Ireland

Adapted from the 9th-century Hilton of Cadboll Stone. *Royal Museum of Scotland, Edinburgh*

Adapted from the 8th-century Aberlemno Cross Slab. *Aberlemno, Angus, Scotland*

Adapted from the 9th-century Hilton of Cadboll Stone. *Royal Museum of Scotland, Edinburgh*

Taken from the 9th-century Shandwick Stone. *Shandwick, Ross and Cromarty, Scotland*

Adapted from the 9th-century Hilton of Cadboll Stone. *Royal Museum of Scotland, Edinburgh*

Interconnecting pattern from the 9th-century Shandwick Stone. *Shandwick, Ross and Cromarty, Scotland*

designs in metalwork

Late 4th-century BC bronze strainer. *British Museum, London*

sixteen

Adapted from a 3rd-century BC iron scabbard. *Musée Municipal, Châlons-sur-Marne, France*

designs in metalwork

Taken from a 3rd–1st-century BC decorated bronze knob, probably from a chariot.
Museum of London

Taken from a 2nd-century BC shield. *British Museum, London*

From a 1st-century bronze mirror, the two small circles with triangles are thought to have been the craftsman's mark. *British Museum, London*

From a 1st-century ornamental horse harness. *British Museum, London*

1st-century bronze mirror from Trelan Bahow, Cornwall. *British Museum, London*

twenty-two

From a 1st-century ornamental horse harness. *British Museum, London*

designs in metalwork

A Celtic triskelion pattern found on a 1st-century tin-plated, bronze plaque.
British Museum, London

twenty~four

Taken from a 1st-century horse trapping. *British Museum, London*

From a 1st-century ornamental horse harness. *British Museum, London*

From a 1st-century Desborough bronze mirror. *British Museum, London*

Design from a 2nd-century BC bronze scabbard. *Ulster Museum, Belfast*

twenty-eight

From a 2nd–1st-century BC round shield boss found in the River Thames.
British Museum, London

designs in metalwork

From a 6th– 8th-century lead decorated disc. *National Museum of Scotland, Edinburgh*

Adapted from an enamelled decoration on a 6th-century hanging bowl. *Herbert Museum and Art Gallery, Coventry, England*

Taken from the 8th-century Blackwater shrine. *Ulster Museum, Belfast, Northern Ireland*

From a 6th-century hanging bowl mount. *British Museum, London*

Decoration from a 6th-century brooch fastening. *National Museum of Ireland, Dublin*

thirty-four

Design from a 6th-century disc-head pin. *British Museum, London*

Taken from the 8th-century Blackwater shrine. *Ulster Museum, Belfast, Northern Ireland*

designs in metalwork

Taken from the 8th-century Blackwater shrine. *Ulster Museum, Belfast, Northern Ireland*

Detail from a 7th-century silver and enamel plaque. *National Museum of Scotland, Edinburgh*

Design taken from an 8th-century die. *Private collection*

Taken from the 8th-century Blackwater shrine. *Ulster Museum, Belfast, Northern Ireland*

Copper alloy disc from an 8th–9th-century house-shaped shrine. *Museo Civico Medievale, Bologna, Italy*

Forty-one

From a 6th–7th-century enamel bronze mount from a hanging bowl. *Sheffield City Museum, England*

Forty-two

From an 8th-century Christian bronze belt shrine. *National Museum of Ireland, Dublin*

From the 8th-century Tara Brooch. *National Museum of Ireland, Dublin*

FORCY~FOUR

From an 8th-century bronze belt buckle. *National Museum of Ireland, Dublin*

designs in metalwork

From the 8th-century Tara Brooch. *National Museum of Ireland, Dublin*

forty-six

From an 8th-century bronze belt buckle. *National Museum of Ireland, Dublin*

designs in illuminated manuscripts

forty-seven

Taken from the 7th-century Book of Durrow. *Trinity College, Dublin*

forty-eight

From a large decorative panel from the 7th-century Lindisfarne Gospels.
British Library, London

forty-nine

Taken from the 8th-century Lichfield Gospels. *Lichfield Cathedral Chapter Library, Lichfield, England*

Taken from the 8th-century Canterbury Codex Aureus. *Kungliga Biblioteket, Stockholm*

designs in illuminated manuscripts

Taken from the 9th-century Book of Kells. *Trinity College, Dublin*

From the 9th-century Book of Kells. *Trinity College, Dublin*

fifty-three

Taken from the 7th-century Book of Durrow. *Trinity College, Dublin*

FIFTY-FOUR

Taken from the 7th-century Lindisfarne Gospels. *British Library, London*

Taken from the 8th-century Lichfield Gospels. *Lichfield Cathedral Chapter Library, Lichfield, England*

Taken from the 8th-century Canterbury Codex Aureus. *Kungliga Biblioteket, Stockholm*

fifty–seven

Taken from the 9th-century Book of Kells. *Trinity College, Dublin*

fifty-eight

Taken from the 9th-century Book of Kells. *Trinity College, Dublin*

fifty~nine

Design from the 7th-century Book of Durrow. *Trinity College, Dublin*

designs in illuminated manuscripts

Taken from the 7th-century Lindisfarne Gospels. *British Library, London*

sixty~one

Taken from the 8th-century Lichfield Gospels. *Lichfield Cathedral Chapter Library, Lichfield, England*

sixty-two

Spiral roundel with knotwork from the 9th-century Book of Kells. *Trinity College, Dublin*

Taken from the 9th-century Book of Kells. *Trinity College, Dublin*

sixty~four

Design from the 7th-century Book of Durrow. *Trinity College, Dublin*

designs in illuminated manuscripts

sixty–five

Taken from the 7th-century Lindisfarne Gospels. *British Library, London*

Taken from the 8th-century Lichfield Gospels. *Lichfield Cathedral Chapter Library,*
Lichfield, England

sixty~seven

Taken from the 9th-century Book of Kells. *Trinity College, Dublin*

Taken from the 9th-century Book of Kells. *Trinity College, Dublin*

sixty~nine

Design from the 7th-century Book of Durrow. *Trinity College, Dublin*

designs in illuminated manuscripts

Taken from the 9th-century Book of Kells. *Trinity College, Dublin*

designs in illuminated manuscripts

Taken from the 7th-century Lindisfarne Gospels. *British Library, London*

seventy~two

Taken from the 9th-century Book of Kells. *Trinity College, Dublin*

designs in illuminated manuscripts

Taken from the 9th-century Book of Kells. *Trinity College, Dublin*

Design from the 7th-century Book of Durrow. *Trinity College, Dublin*

designs in illuminated manuscripts

Taken from the 9th-century Book of Kells. *Trinity College, Dublin*

Taken from the 9th-century Book of Kells. *Trinity College, Dublin*

Taken from the 7th-century Lindisfarne Gospels. *British Library, London*

seventy-eight

Taken from the 9th-century Book of Kells. *Trinity College, Dublin*

designs in illuminated manuscripts

Taken from the 9th-century Book of Kells. *Trinity College, Dublin*

modern designs

Design by George Bain from his early 20th-century book *Celtic Art – The Methods of Construction*.

Modern spiral tattoo design.

Yin and yang.

Design in the style of the Book of Durrow.

eighty-four

Inspired by a cross slab design. *Gallon Priory, Co. Offaly, Ireland*

Based on the 8th-century Phoenix Park openwork mount. *National Museum of Ireland, Dublin*

Adapted from various spirals in the style of the 8th-century Gospel of St Chad.

Adapted from George Bain's *Celtic Art – The Methods of Construction.*

Adapted from St Vigean's stone, Arbroath, Angus, Scotland.

eighty~nine

Adapted from the Book of Kells.

Adapted from St Vigean's stone, Arbroath, Angus, Scotland.

ninety~one

Adapted from St. Vigean's stone, Arbroath, Angus, Scotland.

Tribal heart design.

Adapted from the decorations on early Celtic swords.

modern designs

Loosely based on a 7th-century hanging bowl. *British Museum, London*

Adapted from a carved stone cross.

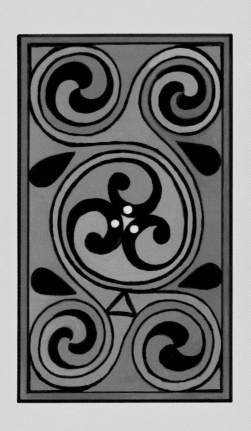

Design idea from a carved stone cross.

Based on a design on a 7th-century stone cross.

Triskelion pattern created from various sources.

Spiral design surrounded by dogs' heads taken from the Lindisfarne Gospels.

one hundred

Adapted from a design in a 7th-century Gospel book.

Triangular spiral with knotwork centre.

Books by Courtney Davis

The Celtic Saint Book,
Blandford Press, 1995

Celtic Image,
Blandford Press, 1996

Celtic Ornament: Art of the Scribe,
Blandford Press, 1996

Celtic Initials and Alphabets,
Blandford Press, 1997

Celtic Illumination: The Irish School,
Thames and Hudson, 1998

Celtic Tattoo: Workbook One,
Awen Press, 2002

Celtic Tattoo: Workbook Two,
Awen Press, 2003

Viking Tattoo: Workbook,
Awen Press, 2003

More information and examples of the art of Courtney Davis
can be found at: **www.celtic-art.com**

Bibliography

Symbolism of the Celtic Cross,
Derek Bryce, Llanerch Enterprises, 1989

Celtic Design: A Sourcebook of Patterns and Motifs,
Iain Zaczek, Studio Editions, 1995

Celtic Art: The Methods of Construction,
George Bain, Constable, 1951

Celtic Art In Pagan and Christian Times,
J. Romilly Allen, Bracken Books, 1993

Lindisfarne Gospels,
Janet Backhouse, Phaidon Press, 1981

The Book of Kells,
Bernard Meehan, Thames and Hudson, 1994

The Book of Kells,
Peter Brown, Thames and Hudson, 1980

Celtic and Anglo Saxon Painting,
Carl Nordenfalk, Chatto and Windus, 1977